REFLECTION ON DOTS

Vern Fein

ISBN: 978-81-19228-07-2

First Edition: 2023
Rs. 200/-

Cyberwit.net
HIG 45 Kaushambi Kunj, Kalindipuram
Allahabad - 211011 (U.P.) India
http://www.cyberwit.net
Tel: +(91) 9415091004
E-mail: info@cyberwit.net

DEDICATION: Again, for my second book my gratitude has not changed for the support, help, and inspiration from my wife, Ilyse, and my three children, Adam. Seth, and Erin, all artists in their own right. Also to my two superb poetry groups: The Champaign-Urbana Poetry Group and the one from Rat's Ass Review.

THOUGHTS ON POETRY: I did not write a poem until I was 75 when one just poppsd into my head. It is in this volume entitled—FAIRY TALE DAUGHTER. Soon after came another poem from this collection—FISHING. Poems began coming to me like birds landing in a tree, I found some fellow travellers who have given me excellent input on every poem I have ever published. Now poetry has become a true delight in my retired life and I am so glad to share it with others and read aloud at special community events. I hope this second round of my warbling will also be pleasing to you. I have no muse. My Muse is the world of poetry itself.

"For every poet, it is always morning in the world; history, a forgotten insomniac nightmare. The fate of poetry is to fall in love with the world, in spite of History." Derek Walcott

Contents

I. TURNING LIVES OVER

CALUMET CITY

How does a tiny town triple every weekend
as if people were stuffed into it?
It ballooned into riotous noise, laughter
pumped full of sin—Little Las Vegas.
We teen boys stopped our red truck
before the open door of a strip joint,
pretended it stalled to get a glimpse
of the naked flesh until the doorman chased us
around the block to try again later.

We had Uncle Art, big rings on his fingers,
the rich relative, owner of three taverns:
The Circus Tap: Where spinning a wheel of fortune got you a free drink if you were on the right stool, a painting of a scantily clad lady riding a tiger staring at you.
The Little Club: Where our Father cajoled our Step-Mother from country music to his bed.
Art's Dog House: Where oodles of Kewpie dogs were stuck in every crevice, begging for a drink.

Art bought a handgun, twirling it on his fat finger
in our living room, not removing the yellow tag.
"I'm not paying those fucking Dagos
another dime for their damn protection."
My Father: "You're crazy Art; they'll kill you.
You can't protect yourself."

The gun, with the yellow tag still on it,
was found by his body, riddled by bullets,

the newspapers called a robbery.
We teen boys took our friends past his house
where his widow lived to marvel
at the plastered-over bullet holes in the garage,
making us big shots in the neighborhood.

Returned years later to that razed section of town,
taverns resplendent with neon replaced
by ill-painted, sagging warehouses,
bent spears of grass growing between cracks
in the sidewalks that once had danced,
the only town that gladly lowered the number
on its green population sign.

JEANNE AND SHIRLEY

Young girl friends of mine
before the sex claw
pinched and scratched.

Sweet Jeanne.
Afternoons spent together on your screened-in porch,
talking for hours, dabbling in youth.
You cried when I beat you
in the Spelling Bee.
I cried because you cried.
We held hands when your Dad died.

Wild Shirley.
An imaginary horse, I chased
you around the playground.
Skipped lunch with you,
ran through fields of daffodils,
wove crowns for our heads.

Jeanne, we were teens
when I saw you working in a department store.
Your dyed hair unrecognizable,
face thick with makeup, lip gloss,
barely able to restrain the disdain
for your nerdy friend.
Turned to a phantom customer
when I greeted you.

Shirley, a cheerleader, moved to another school,
embarrassed when I said hello.
Your makeup pancaked me,
friends gossiped your reputation.
Ran away as fast as you could
from your nerdy friend,
cartwheeling my heart.

Were we to find ourselves
in rockers now,
miraculously living
in the same old folks' home,
would we be friends again?

HEEBIE JEEBIES

Twelve years old,
enthralled by Jan August's *Misirlou,*
I listen to the 78 record on my phonograph.
My heart soars with the strings.

I notice a stack of 45's
with bright, colored centers
my Father brought home from his tavern,
donated by the jukebox man.

I never heard of Little Richard,
put on the white and gold label.

I got the heebie jeebies 'cause I love you so

My heart beats faster,
feet dance.

Next weekend, a teen party.
Over the loudspeaker—

Tutti Frutti, oh rootie

Little Richard again.

At home, the 78's,
Patti Page, Rosemary Clooney,
Johnnie Ray, Frankie Laine,
lay scattered on the floor.

Instead the record player spins
Rock Around the Clock,
Rock N' Roll Is Here To Stay,
Maybellene, Blueberry Hill.

Violins got heebie jeebied.
78's collected dust.

Little Richard—
piercing wail, pounding piano,
towering pompadour, raunch and religion—
with Chuck Berry, Fats Domino
broke the sound barrier
for the rest of my life.

CARBON MAN

Roped into a summer job
as a railroad yard clerk
before college
before novels, poetry
consumed my time.

Money chose a summer job.

Real fear
to be with
real men,
underscored
my first day
when an engineer
screamed at me,
a carload
of Lincoln-Continentals,
decapitated,
routed on the wrong track.
But it was the previous
clerk's mistake.

Relieved until
the Boss said:
"Watch out kid!
At night when
you're walking
between the cars
recording numbers:

Old Ralph
decapitated,
a piece of board sticking out."

Covering vacations
by the regulars
I switched jobs
every two weeks
until early August,
spent a month as a carbon man.

After forty years,
Joe got sick,
extra time off,
the Boss said:
"It's your job now, kid.
Easy.
Insert one of three carbon sheets
into piggyback lading bills,
three, five, seven.
That's all you do all day,
what Joe did all day.
For forty years."

What is Joe like?
"Doesn't talk much,
just did his job.
Loves his wife, beer, the Cubs
in that order.
No kids."
Said the Boss.

Forty years
stuffing carbons.
I developed my own system.
For variety,
an hour of threes,
hour of fives,
hour of sevens.
Repeat. Repeat.
Sometimes in reverse order.

Time crawled
through August.
Joe came back.
Thanked me:
"How'd you like my job?"
I couldn't ask:
How can you stuff carbons
for forty years
not run screaming
toward the tracks?

Soon in college,
I read Hamlet:
To be or not to be?
A carbon man.
I made my choice.
Realized my luck.
I am sorry
men still stuff.

EYES LOCK

He said his wife wept
as they walked down the aisle
lined by beds at the Children's Home
in Ethiopia, there to adopt.
Row after row of smiling or tearful faces.
Her eyes locked on those of a small child.
She turned to him and gushed:
"This is our daughter!"

When my wife and I drove to Indiana
for a dog rescue, row after row
of cages with pleading eyes,
she said their eyes locked
and Butter became our precious pet.

Where would adoptees
end up if eyes had not locked?

I say a prayer for the children
and the dogs who did not
lock eyes.

OUR ANCESTOR, SIR JAMES

Always proud of our family,
Mom sought ways to make us special.
Regaled us about Sir James of our lineage.
Preserved a news clipping about this legend.

She'd squint her eyes and say:
Made the English Navy the greatest in the world,
ruler of the seven seas.
Maybe greater than Sir Francis.
Darn history books couldn't figure that out.

Scurvy, lack of vitamin C, made you weak,
bleeding gums, pain in your limbs, even death.
If a sailor with scurvy fought
against a sailor who didn't, no chance.
A scurvied crew could languish a ship,
make it into prey, lose the battle.

Our Lancaster ancestor, Sir James
was the smart one,
just like you kids,
and your poor passed Father.
He brought lemons and limes
on board in barrels.
The English sailors, called limeys,
sucked them,
other nations didn't know any better.
Made England the mistress of the high seas.
We never knew if it was apocryphal.
I kept the clipping in my wallet
until it got washed in the laundry.

Sir James faded, but his memory lives on.
Lemon wedges in my water,
lime twisting in my gin.

WHY I FELL OUT OF LOVE WITH DEBBIE REYNOLDS

My Stepmother worshipped movie magazines.
She wanted to be a star,
almost auditioned for Gene Autry
with her country band,
The Apple Blossom Trio,
but a member got pneumonia
and the cowboy never saw her.

She married my Father,
under the safe umbrella of his adultery,
shading her eyes from what was obvious to all,
Hollywood dreams, the slick pages of those mags
muting her pain.
She left those glossies lying around.

A curious teen,
I took them to my bedroom
and fantasized over and over like all boys do
eyeing the ingenue Debbie Reynolds
as The One.

There was an actual diminutive girlfriend Bonnie,
heart trysts with Margaret O' Brien and Shirley Temple,
later Sandra Dee,
but sparkling Debbie sang and danced
her way into my heart and libido
more than any of them.
She was Tammy and I was in love.

I grew up, went to college.
Dad and Stepmother divorced.
The VietNam War started.
I got radical, marched and protested,
read the Guardian instead of the Hollywood Star.

One day flipping through that Leftist rag
beautiful Debbie's picture danced off the page.
My heart remembered her,
my teen angst throbbed.
I knew vaguely of her bad marriage to Eddie,
how Liz Taylor cleopatraed her,
America's sweetheart trashed like my Step-Mother.
The caption skewered Debbie, complained
she owned 2,000 pairs of shoes and buying more.
Said she wanted to own the world's largest collection.

2,000 pairs—pumps, espadrilles, kitten heels,
winklepickers, ankle straps—etc., etc.
Silver, mauve, yellows, turquoise, reds,
a rainbow of shoe colors,
a display of wanton, uncaring wealth,
shoes of clay.

Ms. Reynolds was still attractive in that photo,
the dazzling, dimpled smile faintly there.
I remembered my crush.
But the web of the Tender Trap was rent.
My heroes now Che and Fidel,
she the enemy, the ruling class.

A child of poverty,
did Debbie forget that no one dated her

because she didn't know how to dress,
wore ratty jeans, a country shirt and tennies?
Is that what made her feet crave
the feel of slipping on shoes,
one after the other
while children starved?

Debbie is gone now,
stroked out the day after her beloved daughter died.
What kind of shoes did she wear in her coffin?

I fell out of love and into reality.
I fell in love with my wife,
marches and protests,
moccasins,
beside my own worn down boots.

PORTRAITS OF GRAN OLLIE

Dorian Gray should have painted your portrait.

I
You told marvelous stories to us,
your grandsons,
tales of Candyland and disparate animals,
cat and walrus, pig and elephant, horse and snake,
woven on the spot.

II
Our Mother told us your tale.
You were lost as a child in St. Louis,
found at a Convent and spirited to Arkansas.
You were betrothed to a German exchange student,
who was murdered by an unrequited yokel love.
You married the yokel's best friend.
Mom was born.
The best friend lasted only a year, never seen again.

III
At first, you were a lady barber, then danced across Vaudeville.
Smoking red hair lit up an insurance man.
Wild romance wed John Barleycorn
you liquored your way across the South until the Crash.
Harold—Hoovered— took his own life.

IV
Mom moved North to marry a Yankee.
You followed and told us the stories
except on the nights you mumbled and stank.

We didn't know a bottle had a different genie.

V
Our Father was an abusive Lothario,
scoldings and beatings to cover his guilt.
You and Mom fled to an Aunt and Uncle in the middle of the night.
Father pursued in rage.
Farmer Bill, blocking the door, threatened:
"Remember Yankee; I butcher my own hogs."

VI
After years of penury you wed Henry,
the happy cab driver who loved you well
until he died of intractable cancer-colored pain.

VII
Then, the clock of time stroked.
I visited you throughout,
prayed for you and talked to you, grasping a bony hand,
only your eyes able to move,
blinking yes and no until you died,
a stark look of amazement plastered on your face.

VIII
Years later, my own grandboys begged a story,
two little boys, mouth agape,
like birds grasping for words.
You showed up in the room
gray hair, flower print dress, without a bottle,
smiling out the words for me.

GRANDMA CRIED

Grandma lost her second husband,
the saint, from a sudden heart attack,
not the scalawag, who walked out the door
when Mom was two.
The first one broke Grandma's heart leaving,
the second one broke her heart dying.

Grandma did not shed a tear,
but when the funeral was over,
when TAPS and the gun salute faded,
she jumped in the grave,
hugged and hugged the casket
until they dragged her away,
her face as hard
as the Brass around her.

Home they went,
no tears, Grandma a Sphinx
who sat in the house,
zombied through her days,
mechanically cleaned.
Frail as a bird,
Mom couldn't flap a wing,
wheedled and pleaded
for Grandma to cry.

One day, the statue stood stark still.
Mom said she did not know
what moved her to strike.

But she slugged Grandma,
smacked her right in the jaw.
Her mother looked at her stunned,
scrunched up her face
and wailed for days.

Mom and Grandma,
the best shoulders
for each other
the rest of their lives.

DAMN YOU, CHUBBY CHECKER

Silky ballroom dancers, my folks also loved the jitterbug.
I took to that jive and won contests, gyrated my way through my teens
into girls' hearts and arms, straight through American Bandstand,
college, and a job teaching my art to all-girls' PE classes.

Also taught the heavyweight wrestling champion from our school
who bear-hugged me in gratitude because he was able to dance
with his sweetie at Homecoming, well worth the twenty-five cents
an hour
I charged him to practice at the mirror with his dorm room doorknob.

I was a star, the Cab Calloway of my small Midwestern college,
until along came Chubby and my life got suddenly Twisted,
forced to practice with a towel and swing my butt back and forth—
the magic of the jitterbug gone, a wallflower dance master now.

No one touched each other anymore.
No hand holding, no cool twirls or Ricky Nelson slides.
You could twist with yourself. You could twist with a group.
No one needed to teach you if towel swivels convinced the mirror.
Dull anonymity. Damn you, Checker!

DIALOGUE WITH A TROPICAL FISH

My wife dragged me to a birthday party where I knew no one.
I noticed a fish, alone, glaring in the tank behind me,
a beautiful, black angel fish.

"I know you," she said.
"You kill my sisters and brothers, throw baited hooks at them,
ignore their staring eyes, butcher them even when still alive.
You would do that to me, but no one catches tropical fish.
If we were not small and beautiful and could be eaten,
you would swing hooks before us, reel us in triumph."

I fought back: "I love tropical fish,
hope my retirement includes the Great Barrier reef,
colorful art gallery in the ocean.
I would love to swim with them."

But I could deny nothing, thought of the tackle box I got for
Father's Day,
celebrative family fish dinners, vacations to the lake, a tradition
from my Father,
fat stringer pictures on my computer gallery.

I knew I would not change.
I wanted to tell her that's just the way the world is,
plead my humanity.

My wife brought me a drink, pulled me toward someone
I will never remember.

The angel turned her back, swam away.

BLIND RAY

Ray was totally blind,
wheelchair-bound, eager to please,
happy for companionship.
I thought I was just a grad volunteer,
there to read, do my bit for humanity,
but Ray shared his poems and prose with me,
proud smile, craved approval for his work.

The misspellings overwhelmed,
grammar—bad on bad.
Plotless rambles. Unfree verse.
Ray talked incessantly.
He often had a cold,
snot hung from his nose,
sickened my stomach.
I could not praise.
I could not look at him.
Mumbled: "Interesting."

Given my literary standards,
his chronic congestion,
I just disappeared.
Ignored his calls,
cries on the machine:
Where are you?

Youth can be a bonfire
of good intentions.

Guilt decades later
embered a cold heart.

What if Ray instead had been
Renee, a red-headed beauty
who wrote stirring poems,
smile gentle as a dove?
So I fell in love,
married her, had three children
who grew up to help the world,
allowed us to see the beauty of life.

But he was Ray
and I left.

HISTORY OF SPANKING

Mrs. Furness, my second grade teacher,
long dead now, told my mother,
"If I believed in geniuses, he is one."
Made me her pet, skinny me, buck teeth,
owl glasses, unruly cowlick,
left in charge of the class
when Mrs. F. went to the Ladies Room.

Watched over her desk, stopped
kids from messing around.
Janie did, despite my protests,
stuck out her tongue.
Class clown, tipped over
the inkwell on all the papers,
fled to her desk just in time.

"Who did this!." screeched Mrs. F.
"Who did this!," spit my name.

I was mute. Janie and the class
prayed I would not tattle.

What would the kids do?
Push me off the monkey bars?
Flip me off the Teeter-Totter?
Refuse to play?
Billy once spit on Stuart.

Mrs. F., arms akimbo, glared:
"Either you tell who
or I call your Father."
Terror squeaked out, "Janie."

She dragged her up front,
flashed her ruler, whipped her,
ripped her dress,
sent her to the office,
the class yelled, cried, glared.

It is said: Spare the rod, spoil the child.
And they spanked, switched
and whipped, even beat
until Dr. Spock—the Dr. Suess for butts—
said: Wrong thing to do.

In Texas, they allow paddling again.
Triumphant Mrs. F., arms akimbo,
smiles down from above.

SEEING MY BROTHER OFF

Drop my 79 year old younger brother off
at the local airport, small and unstable
like an old stagecoach stop,
sending him to California to join
in the celebration of his son's 50th.

Remember my first flight
on a prop plane to visit
our divorced mom in Rhode Island,
the tower telling the pilot
to bank around again because
he forgot to drop the landing gear.
My brother won't have to deal with that
on this memory trip to the Golden state.

But I made it and he made it,
he a stint spying on Vietnamese
in a War he came to hate,
as I, stateside, wore my boots down
protesting that atrocity.

He became a skilled carpenter,
building monuments of furniture
in homes all over the area.
I taught special ed children,
making them special despite the ed.

Now both with fifty-year marriages,
we fish in a local lake,

root for different teams,
bond in a local poetry club,
turning our long lives into verse.

Aches and pains travel with him,
heart, iron, energy, leg problems,
but he rolls on as we always have,
fighting through the age
that ain't for sissies.

We realize we are close to sending
each other on a final flight
from which we won't return,
joining the angels who will make sure
the landing gear is down,
accepting our forever wings.

TRAVELS WITH MY AUNT

Aunt hauled me around
with her on her adventures

when I was young.
She was a free bird,

never had a real job,
only errands for her successful

mother and older brother, and,
my parents preoccupied with their lives,

a father busy with adultery,
a step-mother hiding in movie magazines,

left me at loose ends.
Aunt Elaine thought I was bright,

she stimulated my mind
in ways no one else did.

Always stacks of books by her bed side;
I think she read the whole library.

But pages would be turned only until a book bored her,
like the half-smoked butts she squashed, filling her ashtrays.

On the adventures in her world—
the zoo, baseball games, hole-n the wall eateries—

we visited champion bowlers who were lesbians,
she a closet one I found out years later.

Never married but verbally abused
her one boyfriend (her shield)

because he was a pro-union liberal,
snidely calling him her Comrade.

She read Marx but was a Republican
who loved Eisenhower, loathed Adlai.

Dressed like and was a beatnik
before they were named,

always wore dark sunglasses,
even inside, sported a tam,

frequented bars with peanuts on the floor,
quipping until her humor turned

the bar flies' laughter into scorn
as her words became mocking fire,

forged by her boiling anger.
Too often I was the target of her ire.

The last time I saw her
when a young family man

who visited her only because
I felt her loneliness over the phone,

she was sloppy into a crying jag,
taking shots from a variety

of schnapps bottles, a rainbow of flavors,
getting drunker and drunker,

pounding the table over and over,
crying and moaning harder and harder

for every failure
in the world and her life.

Why did I continue to see her?
Why did I tell you her broken story?

Because I know she loved me
and, indeed, I loved her too.

MY WIFE IS ALWAYS SINGING

As if she were a bird in disguise.
she looks like the woman I married,
maybe a different kind of a bird now—
not a blue bird but a partridge—
older now, feathers graying
she still sings much of the day.

It was song that won my heart
when she played her guitar
and I first noticed her beauty,
her smile and her voice.
She usually sings in our kitchen now,
but songs all around the house
day and night, personal vespers
burst out with all the lyrics.

Saying she is a bit absent-minded
which indeed is true, a family chuckle,
she impeccably remembers all the lyrics
of those songs to me, our children, and God
which spring forth like bird rituals.

Now in old age, she still sings,
even as we read side by side.

I expect she will sing at her own funeral
before she nests and warbles forever.

LURKER

On my daily walk
in my neighborhood,
cuddled houses,
trimmed, green lawns,
saluting soldier trees,
manicured flower beds,
my dog and I stroll
past a gnarled tree,
twisted, a runt,
bony fingers sky pointed,
green moss dusted
on her wrinkled bark.
Misfit body.
A witch alive
in the burbs.

AM I INTELLIGENT?

An article appeared on Yahoo,
unusual attributes of high intelligence.
Ah, I can test myself against the world.
How will I fare?

To start, I am the oldest child,
a leg up, but no choice of mine
and I did take piano lessons,
but failed miserably.

I have owned cats, don't now,
but had a lot of cats
so I must be super curious,
even though it has not killed me.

Alas, I am not left-handed.
There must be far less
intelligent people than I thought.
And I am not tall.
Wasn't Napoleon short?
Do I begin to question this list?
Roll on.

I read at a young age,
was read to and memorized books
to delight the adults.
And I have always been
very anxious, taking pills for years.

Yes, a sense of humor,
even laugh at my own jokes.
And I am quite disorganized.
Can't even find my lists!

Eschew luck, one of my
cats was witch black and
I fear no ladders or mirrors.
Don't know if my Mother
breast-fed me. Too old
to remember, but must have
since this list is going my way.

Definitely a night owl,
reading lamp on till late.
Viewed as lazy as a child.
Only read comic books for years
and watched the Cubs,
avoided every odious chore.
But very focused,
perhaps OCD for a middle name.

Admit when I am wrong,
though not frequently.
Am not at all the strong silent type,
more a gadfly with a mouth.
Does that disqualify me?

But I seem to be lining up quite well?
What do you think?
I love challenges
and of course I multitask,
see life as a big stove

where I manage many burners,
but I am not a good cook—
not on the list though.

Surround myself with smart people
who have me around for the same reason
and married a smart woman
though she goes to bed early
and hates cats.

Egads! Intelligent people
shun electronics.
Can you fail at one category
and be eliminated?
Are there levels of intelligence?
Perhaps I am just smart, not highly?

But I am empathetic,
love facts, am a perfectionist,
keep a top the news,
carefully examine my ideas
over and over with my
Rubik's cube mind
and, in truth,
don't think I am smart
even though this wonderful test
says otherwise.
What do you think?

FIRST ACID TRIP

Hey, I saw a photo of us
when we were young and beautiful
like the magic world
that found us lying on the bed
during our first acid trip
rainbow colors
mixed with soundz
side-splitting laughter.

First you said the Hamm's bear
from the Sky Blue commercial
was in your socks—
almost howled them off.

Tried to recall the words
to Hickory Dickory Dock
and got it wrong—
did the mouse run up or down—
we laughed ourselves to sleep.

Those were the Days my friend
we thought they'd never end

But cats came on the scene
cut the pills for profit,
drove us hippies
out of our synaesthetic dreams.

Soon our hitchhiking minds
only took bad trips
and poof the magic.

ONION MEMORIES

My brother and I travelled to see our property,
our only inheritance. That land was the one thing
our wicked stepmother could not finagle.

We go there ritually every summer
to look it over, see about repairs
as if we were truly businessmen,
not the artists we became.
We need to sign a new lease every five years,
protect the annual stipend for our children.

It is now a tire repair business,
was a Standard Oil before
the tavern we lived in during our childhood
was torn down after Dad's heart attack.

As we walk around the old building inspecting,
we look at the down-turned shopping center
behind the property, half empty now, and recall
when it was just onion fields as far as you can see
and remember the almost naked and dirty
Mexican children who roamed all summer,
stacked the onions, coming by at dusk to play.

I remember a young girl with no top on
though she was old enough for one,
her buds arousing me and my curiosity
about why her parents would allow that.

Our mother said they were farm workers,
forced to pick onions every year for a pittance
because they were so poor—cheap labor.

When I looked out on the dilapidated shopping mall,
I realize they are either dead or perhaps
their children are refugees many reject,
like the onions that rotted in the racks,
thrown away, wasted, so machines
pick and stack them now.

YER OUT!

Once the best fun, baseball cards—
sacred for poor, working-class boys
before we could afford to go to a real game,
before TV.

Collected cards, a big deal and cheap.
We could stuff boxes full
all the stars along with the bench jockeys,
shuffle fantasies before our eyes,
each face our own miracle catch or towering home run.

In the winter, when snow and ice pinned us inside,
we made a game with them.
Placed the cards on the floor,
each player in his right position,
even a catcher.
Our own All-star team, changed line-ups.

We were the managers!
Teams took turns.
With our index finger, we flicked the batter card
across the wooden bedroom floor,
a dirt diamond in our minds.

Whereever it landed determined the play.
Hit another card—out!
Land clean, a hit, depended how far it flew.
A home run was a top the heating vent.

Rooted for our favorite team.
Pirates, Reds, Cubbies!
Charted the league standings.
Nine innings, whiling away winter.
Played for hours until our cuticles bled
from snapping floating heroes into the air.
Heal in a few days—Batter up!

We had no idea of value—Cokes were a nickel.
We did not know American greed
would soon make some cards—
Williams, DiMaggio, Mantle—
if we did not bend or crinkle them,
worth enough to pay for college fees.

Comic books, then girls, took over.
The cards sat in a box in the attic,
buried in an Easter basket with fake green grass,
looked more like a field than the old, brown floor.

A small attic fire incinerated them.
Childhood dreams up in smoke.

Years later, our own children collected cards:
"Mom, Dad, buy boxed sets and keep them.
They'll be worth a ton!"
Good parents stored safely,
not in an attic,
cellophane intact
like rare books with perfect spines.

Years later, a surfeit of cards—
America knew her business.
Everyone collected and saved everything.
The market crashed.
Like a player who slid past second base—
"Yer Out"!

STEENY

We called him by his last name,
never Reggie.
Just Steeny
or “Steeny Weenie.”
Back in the 50’s before geek
became a word for uncool or nerd,
before Dylan glorified GEEK
in Ballad of A Thin Man,
Steeny was the object of our taunts,
the bullying we all did
before that was a word anyone cared about.
I jumped in too,
feeling icky inside
when I helped pile on the abuse,
always in a group, never alone
when we pummeled him.

He just took it,
no expression reflected from his coke-bottle glasses,
no hand to his hair when we mocked his cowlick,
just moved on down the hall,
used his locker door as a shield sometimes.

O, that Halloween night.
Boy, did we have a lot of candy!
A surfeit of sugar in all forms.
Still soaped windows,
left lit bags of shit
on porches when we rang the bell,

watched the furious owner
stomping his shoes dirty.
Devil boys.

That night, bulging bags.
I had to carry mine with two hands.
Around the corner, Steeny.
Alone, bag full.
Like piranha we attacked,
ripped the bag from his hands and ran.
"Steeny Weenie.
Steeny Weenie."
Only then did we hear
the night-shattering sob.

Now, as my daughter weeps,
shakes before me, her own bully demons
pulsing in her heart,
do I remember Steeny.

NUMBERS

My daughter struggles with a Statistics class,
complains about probabilities,
sends shudders of memories through me.

In old age now, I don't do numbers,
only see the ball scores,
know the higher number means a win.
Praise to James Van Tassel for the calculator.

In eighth grade, the math teacher,
nicknamed Rajah,
huge in voice and demand,
threatened to call my father
because I didn't pay attention.
Tried to tell him I didn't get it.

What mathematical de Sade
invented Algebra?
Saved by Mr. Piazza
the wrestling coach, a D minus
kept me on the team.

And Mr. Olson for Geometry,
Euclid rhymes with putrid.
He assigned everyone a personal theorem.
So, when he called on me, I always got it right.
Vertical angles are always equal.

In college, took a general Math requirement,
had to pass to stay in school,
had a crush on the tutor,
tried hard to please beautiful Ms. Christiansen,
No one in the world has gotten a
D minus, minus—except me.

On the LSAT for grad school,
the Math exam stumped me
after six problems, ending with a question
about Napoleon's Bones math concept,
equilateral nightmare.
Fifteen minutes in, I put my head down.
The proctor asked: "Are you sick, young man?"

Learned helplessness, they call it,
born with that malady.
I am not proud.
How can you be proud of what you didn't want to be?

But I got smart, married
a woman who could measure things,
took the measure of me.
I made it through life without numbers.
Can you beat those odds?

THE HELPER

At my in-laws reunion
we lounge in Paradise,
the Pacific a blue shawl tossed over the shoulders
of a mansion surveying
endless clouds, sunbathers, yachts.
We eat, drink, laugh, hug.
One of the children
who flit around the patio
like multi-colored butterflies,
spills something dark
on one of the pristine, white stones,
hand-cut patio slab.

Their hired Latina helper,
an aged lady,
ignores the party around her,
quickly slips from the shadows,
falls on her knees,
slaves hard to restore
purity to that stone,
scrubs and scrubs.
It won't come off.
There is lots of stepping around her.

BLUE ROCK

Once when the world was new,
too pristine for coin, nothing minted,
people gathered shells, stones,
bartered for necessities.

Flash forward to yesterday,
millions of years later.
We have money now,
love of it the root of all evil.

A little girl found a blue rock.
She thought it was pretty.
She rolled it around in her hand,
pretended it was a jewel,
a truly valuable jewel.

Came the sound of an ice cream truck.
Ding a ling, bring your money
and buy your joy.

The little girl proffered the blue rock.
She had no money.
The owner smiled down.

He became a small boy in his heart.

She wanted a cone.

He gave her a sundae.

She gave him the blue rock.

He offered it back.

DANDELION GREENS

Each spring, food a daily struggle,
our mother snatched scads of dandelions,
shook off the dirt, cut away yellow
Rapunzel heads, washed the abundance,
cooked them down. Bacon on lucky days.

We ate whatever was put before us,
never turned up our dirty noses
at the stringy greens, often on our plates.
"They're healthy," she'd plead,
"good for you growing boys."

Years later, she'd tell us
not to mention the greens,
embarrassed by our blessings.

I did anyway,
got an aghast rib poke,
a wry smile from her.

"Can't eat them anymore,"
she'd retort: "Pesticides."

A TRIBUTE TO MOSS HART'S AUNT KATE

Moss Hart of Camelot and My Fair Lady fame.

Moss, families have one or two eccentrics
and yours had Kate.
She took you to the land of thespian magic
several times a week,
silly giggler at the worst times
when it wasn't even a comedy.
You didn't care, young Moss.

When she set fires,
they locked her up.
You tried to find her a fire escape,
remembered how she
spirited you to the shows
ignited your heart and mind
to make people laugh and sing.

Let's toast the Kates of our families,
the odd among our kin,
take a moment to applaud them,
mine the gold instead of the dross,
turn them loose on the youth,
see what magic appears.

PHONE DAUGHTER

Our daughter moved far West to a city,
travels in one of those bands,
criss-crossing our country
leaves dreams like bread crumbs
to claw her way through
brutal, unforgiving woods.
No sight-seeing,
no Grand Canyon,Yellow Stone,
Mammoth Caves, Carlsbad,
but the insides of clubs,
Slinky Jim's in Piquay, Ohio,
Nub Buster in Atlanta,
Dark Flamingo in Louisiana, Carousel City in Oregon,
names like racehorses.

We visit on the phone a lot,
retired father and traveling daughter,
music for a soul,
talk for hours and hours, traversing the nation and our lives,
sharing memories and motel info or where else she slept,
what she ate, how did that show go,
how big was the crowd, how did merch sell?
Will your tour come our way?
FaceTime, some.

I wonder what it felt like when a father
standing at the edge of his farm
in Pennsylvania
looked and looked

into the horizon
after his daughter and her covered wagon,
headed West to somewhere,
husband, beginning brood of kids,
gear, stuff to survive
and no phone
and no words.

THE GENERATIONAL PAST TIME

An old man, arms crossed,
watches his grandson in Farm League,
remembers thousands of hours
on district ball fields across his life,
Major League, Little League, Colt League
games with his sons,
his daughter's softball,
years of coaching them
and other childrens'
beaming faces, crying (there is)—
slides, home runs, doubles.
steals, triples, strikeouts,
singles, walks, shutouts.

Today, thirty years later,
he watches a grandson
on the same field
he coached his son
to a city championship,
an indelible memory
like the trophy
collecting dust in his office
until his son carries
it to his own home one day.

Watches his grandson,
no curve ball here,
a heater straight to the heart.

LEARNING TO STEAL

A small boy squats beside a road
watches Father, Aunt, Uncle,
powerful then.

A rickety truck rolls by slowly,
the pile of bright red tomatoes jostling each other
to see which could stay on.

The Depression-laden adults
salt-shakers in hand, crouch low
as the truck struggles past, leap on the truck bed,
ride down the road, hidden from the driver by the fruit.

Silently, salting and stuffing tomatoes in their mouths,
until they are distant specks to the little boy,
before they jump off, return, sauntering toward him,
the blood of theft running down
free and laughing chins.

FORGIVENESS

My grandsons drag their tent
across the back yard,
uncover an Eden of garter snakes
roiling, scared,
slithering for safety,
one snatched by my oldest grandson,
grasped and petted
before it wriggled away,
the Curse forgiven.

When I was six,
in front of my house,
an adult garter snake
rose and hissed at me.

Terrified, I screamed
for our Great Dane.
Rowdy roared around the house,
snapped up the innocent snake,
shook it to death
while I sobbed and cheered.

For years, I told that story,
fondly remembering my dog.
Now, when I see my grandson
love and release his snake,
it is my snake
for which I feel.

FAIRY TALE DAUGHTER

You know how princes become frogs?
Our daughter became a dog.
In bed, this morning, side by side,
The huge black puppy in our life.
Petting her hunger for affection,
Licking our bedclothes like confection.
I think of our daughter far away
Spreading her wings to win her day.
Leaving behind her family to sing.
Leaving the dog to fetch and bring.
A dog can become a daughter,
And we can become her parents.
Though it cannot hug the same,
Nor have her eyes and smile,
Or make our birthdays shine.
But a dog can be sublime.
Barking her way into our hearts,
Barking away the pain of parting.

CLASS BEHIND GLASS

I visited the aquarium,
saw all you pretty preeners.
Angels, Tetras, Neons,
Double Reds, Corydoras,
fanning your tails
to the ohs and ahs of the gawkers.

I did not see your brothers
and sisters that wait
for the hook you will never smell,
the blue gill, perch, crappie,
bass, catfish—plebeians
of inland lakes,
who will swim carefree,
until they bite that barb
strain and pull
jump and flop
against their death.

They will never swim in a tank
with colorful grasses, fake diver bubbling,
toy stone castle, food sprinkled
in daily by soft hands,
the sweet hum of the filter,
protecting their delicate lungs.

Do those who can afford to sup
on grouper, snapper, orange roughy,
oysters, lobster, calamari,

get to adore
the prettiest, most delicate
water world debutantes?

I see my reflection in the glass.

RESCUES

Today we rescued a dog.
She is cute, lovable.
Never had a home,
never looked at by anyone
the kind man told us
who rescued Butter
from a wretched cage,
confined by hoarders.

Home now
for the first time
sniffing away loneliness—
                    yard to smell
                    nearby park
                    leash walks
                    toys to hassle
                    laps to snuggle
                    beds to flounce
                    more touches
in a single day than ever.

South of here,
children in cages
crammed together
not even their own,
like dogs on display
at PetSmart.

Separated from family,
crowded, inadequate
clothes
showers
food
attention
touch
love
Indefinite.

My wife and I cannot
stroll into that place
look into imploring eyes
bond
fill out paper work
take a rescue by the hand
perhaps stop at McDonald's
on the way
home.

SANTA LIE

In Granny's secure-as-cooking house, I wait eagerly
for the toys, too young to fret about socks,
know Santa's red suit and white beard will soon appear
as the adults around the tree nudge expectations.

My younger brother and I don't miss Uncle Martin's absence,
glue our eyes to the presents that seem to wiggle under the tree,
impatient to toss their bows aside.

The buzz of small talk blasted by a hearty "Ho, Ho, Ho,"
my brother squeaks with joy like the mouse
in The Night Before Christmas.

My squeal turns to horror when I see Santa's beard.
SCOTCH TAPE!
"It's Uncle Martin. He taped on his beard.
He's not Santa!"

My astonished father's face turns to a scowl, turns to anger,
the piercing cries from my brother chasing Merry from the room.

Guilt and blame from the adults land on me—
Ruined Christmas for your little brother—
make me feel fiery coal and ashes of family addictions
before they were deposited like soot on our legacy.

Santa visited my children every year until
some kid at school said he wasn't real
because a fat man couldn't climb down the chimney.

We all laughed.

SPIN THE BOTTLE

They weren't the three
Macbeth witches—
Diana, Nancy, and Donna,
but they were scary as Hell
when we gathered
in Diana's basement
afternoons during middle-school.

We played with our hormones
as kids have done since man
invented bottles.
Round and round and round—
prayed and wished it would
point to someone who would kiss you,
not point to someone who
would scrunch up her face
and say, "No Way."

The deal was go behind
the big furnace in Diana's basement
so you could do it or not.
No one would know
while the others waited
in the next room,
breathless for their fate.

I spun Diana first,
rangy and tall as a stork,
towered over my scrawny self.

That was easy.
We made a deal
behind the furnace,
pretend to kiss and lie,
like lots of others.

Then Nancy,
who had a big nose—
they called her Nosalich—
children cruel always.
We kissed and did not tell,
glad for no rejection.

Finally, Donna.
She said no to me,
the true witch of the three.
She was the sex pot.
Everyone knew she had done
more than kiss.
Later a baby out of wedlock
when you could still say that.

Wonder if teens in basements now
still spin their futures
behind the furnace of their hearts?

MRS. DERMENT

I am 82 today.
While I cut the lawn,
I remember Mrs. Derment,
my first college landlady
when she was 82.

Walking past those Greek houses,
down those old streets,
fresh-minded new grad student,
I saw her first with her back turned
in an old granny dress,
puffing a push lawn mower,
slight rust on the edge of the blades,
up the ridge of her yard.

She rented me a single room,
board elsewhere
and, new to that town,
became a friend.
I watched *Bonzana* with her,
her wording for that cowboy classic.

Once stumbling back to my room
on a Sunday evening,
a term paper weighing down my head,
she said:
*Young man, (*her name for me)
there's this group called the Beatles
on the Ed Sullivan show. Want to watch it with me?

No, I replied, *I have too much to do,*
robbing myself of an iconic experience
to plumb the depths of Pope's Rape Of The Lock.

I am still fortunate to be able
to cut my lawn with a power mower
and don't know how Mrs. Derment
did with just the old blades.
She died at 89.
I neglected to see her that last year.
I think she is happy though.
Surely there is grass in Heaven.

THE DATE FAIRY

An eight year marriage argument.
Mean and ugly words
spatter like kitchen grease.

Wiggling diaper baby
hangs off her side,
seven year old snot nose
sobs in the corner.

His stolid arms
locked in silence,
angry belly protrudes
low over his belt.

The Date Fairy appears.
No wings or wand.
A sad smile on her face,
a mirror in her hand.

The couple stops raging,
the children hush.

The Fairy holds up the mirror
so all can see.
A light flashes.
The couple is at a table
in a coffee shop.
They've just met.

Coo like pigeons,
they talk and talk.
No words heard
in the mirror,
just smiles, love.
He takes her hand.
She squeezes back.

Mad love that night,
married in a year.
Out popped the snot nose,
soon the hanging diaper,
monster bills and Mother-in-law,
nasty psoriasis,
a mutt found their door,
he didn't want it, she did.
Their words from soft to hard.

The mirror repeats,
stops at the hand squeeze.

The Date Fairy vanishes.

OF PARROTS AND FRIENDS

After my wife's weekly visit with her friend
who has early Alzheimer's, she sheds quiet tears,
I listen to her speak of creeping dissolution.

On our honeymoon, I got to know who I wed,
watched her enjoy a bird show as if the various birds—
pigeons, toucans, cockatoos—could understand, appreciate.

The parrots riding trikes came last as the bells struck noon.
Before those birds finished, the audience rose and fled to their fare.
Not my wife. We stood alone and watched till the last bird was done.
She clapped and clapped as if those parrots knew, could take a bow.

Now she tells me of her friend who paints, stands or bows no more,
just lies glaze-eyed, hand-holding, when only fetal remains,
sympathy falls silent, no clapping heard,
that same heart and kindness, like the brilliant sun
that July day with the birds.

II. POTPOURRI:

LITERATURE, HISTORY/POLITICS, RELIGION, HUMOR, PHILOSOPHY

WHAT WE CAN'T DO

What if one woman and I
were left on the Earth
to propagate the human race?
What if we couldn't invent anything—
from a battery to a rocket,
cure small pox?

Adam and Eve didn't bother
with math or technology,
the ground watered itself,
luscious fruit to pluck,
the Four Rivers pure,
animals best friends.

When they left the Garden,
they needed it all,
progressed into civilization,
the last few hundred years,
bombs, machine guns, tanks,
trains, automobiles planes,
skyrocketing technology,
computers, the Internet, I-Phones,
from agrarian to urban,
plowing to the moon.

I couldn't create any of these things—
a failed bird house in shop class—
my dear wife hardly better.
I write poems,

read on the poetry circuit.
She's a garden artist.
We can't develop a circuit for anything
or a chip,
would never have thought of atoms,
become our hero Salk.
Glad there have been billions
to invent these marvels.

Without the weapons though,
please, without the weapons,
but, it seems, those come with the territory.

RICH SCROOGE

In Memory of Alastair Sims

In A Christmas Carol, Dickens described the holidays as "a good time: a kind, forgiving, charitable, pleasant time: the only time I know of in the long calendar of the year, when men and women seem by one consent to open their shut-up hearts freely, and to think of other people below them as if they really were fellow passengers to the grave, and not another race of creatures bound on other journeys.

Did you ever wonder what Scrooge did after he converted?
Invited God right into his heart and turned it around.

And some fancy ghosts scared him into Christmas.
Indeed, he really knew how to do Christmas well.

Raised Bob Cratchit's salary yearly. Hot coals and punch all winter.
Uncle Scrooge blessed Tiny Tim by paying for his schooling.

Found a high-level apprenticeship for Peter and attended Martha's wedding.
Drank tea and befriended dear Mrs. Cratchit.

Located the "marvelous, wonderful" boy and apprenticed him as a butcher.
Gold crowns for Mrs. Dilber, Christmas presents for her kids.

Sent Fred's Sally to seamstress school. Loaned Fred money to build his business.

Visited Old Joe. Helped him remodel and hire the charlady.

Waltzed every Christmas till he couldn't, then sat on the couch
and clapped.
Ate Christmas dinner with "his sister's boy" every year, fat
turkey and all.

Railed against Poor Workhouses and wretched prison conditions.
Poured money into Ignorance and Want all of his days.

Placed a tombstone above the Fezziwigs:
They danced life the best of all.

Sought out Alice and made peace with her.
Met her every need and were friends till her end.

Why could Old Scrooge, who always got more bread
for everyone from then on, do all of this for humanity?

Because he had money till he died.
May we privileged do as well.

GRATEFUL FOR GENES

Raking up the damn infernal,
eternal leaves and grass
every year without fail
they fall on my heart, brain and breath,
can't even burn the dang things no more
so I do it to make my wife happy
wonder if I will still rake if she goes first
but, sweating and swearing,
now realize at 80 how many
I knew are under the ground
with the colored leaves on top,
red blood, yellow phlegm,
orange juice physic, purple splotches,
wonder if they can hear
the raking and the bitching,
or know how grateful I am
I can still do it at all,
don't have to hire
a neighbor boy yet.

QUIET MIND

Mind: Quit speaking to me!
You are rattling on the way you always prattle
and have done so since I was a child
and in old age still talk incessantly.

You have thought good things and given me good ideas.
You've even helped me write some poems and songs,
suggested I say kind things, but also mean words.

I have meditated to rid myself of your chatter, but you are good
at intruding whenever you want, breaking in like a noisy child.
The world keeps happening, leaping or slugging forward,
throwing new sticks on the fire of my brain
that sparks you into a blaze or just embers.

Even when I sleep you are loud and raucous.
Dreams have dialogue and you have no trouble
speaking up and sometimes dream words are worse.
In them, you have no filters, say what the hell you want
which you can't say when we are awake.
Stuff our dreams with people we forgot
or don't like or love from all times and ages,
even people and things that never existed,
then wake us up and laugh at us as we slowly rise to reality,
unless you just disappear and leave us with wadded bedcovers.

I have not been able to stop you all of my days.
I'm not going to speculate about what you will do
if there is an afterlife. The idea of sharing, speculating,

pontificating, philosophizing for all eternity is more
like a hellish punishment than a heavenly reward.

Maybe then, instead, you will have an angelic
way of finally, truly being quiet, granting peace.

TOLKIEN DIED

Even immortal men are mortal,
a bleeding ulcer and chest infection at 81,
nothing magical, nothing fantastic.

Tolkien did not die when he should have.
Reluctant to serve in WW I,
married, languished in Britain,
family-badgered, socially scorned,
enlisted as a signals officer,
shipped to France.

On the verge
of the Battle of the Somme,
lice ignited raging trench fever.
The prescribed ointment
maddened the lice,
sent him to a British hospital.

His entire battalion
destroyed at the Somme.
Lice saved the Rings.

OF MARGARET WISE BROWN: GOODNIGHT MARGARET

Little one, as I rock you to sleep,
you do not yet know your world.
Your room is blue, not green—
no telephone, red balloon,
or picture of a cow jumping over the moon,
no kittens or mittens, no bears, young mouse.
You have a comb and a brush, a clock, a doll house
and your Grandmother rocking you, hush.

You do not know of Margaret.
I will tell you now and I will tell you later.
You will not understand me now.
Will you understand me later?

Goodnight Brownie:
Beautiful, green-eyed, blonde-haired vixen,
extravagant, eccentric lover of King Juan Carlos,
a John D. Rockefeller nephew,
Ms. Michael Strange, ex-wife of John Barrymore,
others.

Little one, do not kick your leg up in the air
if your doctors tell you no,
clotting your leg and stopping your heart.
Do not give your inheritance to a wastrel.

Instead write 100 picture books
with melodies you can whistle.

Goodnight stars
Goodnight air
Goodnight noises
Goodnight foolish choices
Everywhere.

DEAD BRONTES

Oh, you think I write
of Emily, Charlotte, and Anne,
tragic young deaths,
lives snuffed out
caring for neglectful father Patrick,
wastrel brother Branwell.

No, I tell of older sisters
with forgotten names,
Maria and Elizabeth, who died
at Cowan Bridge School
from hunger and cold.

Patrick spirited the surviving sisters home
to create Jane Eyre, Heathcliff, Agnes Gray,
and assorted poems by fake male authors.

History has a way of raveling.
Ah, but that unraveling leaves life
full of mystery and grief.

This is for you, Maria and Elizabeth.
What might you have penned
had Patrick repented sooner?

BEATING HAWTHORNE TO IT

Herman Melville worked as many jobs as Colonel Sanders,
store and bank clerk, farm hand and teacher,
but none but the sea and whaling
satisfied him into writing the popular *Typee,*
and other novels of the noble savage,
first rejected because the critics
said the tales couldn't be true.

He wrote as deep as Moby Dick
when the white whale plunged,
snatched Ahab's leg and soul.

But fame swam off like the white beast,
flayed by British and American pundits,
sliced and stripped like a dead whale,
never to be enjoyed in his lifetime,
his poetry and *Billy Budd*
drowning in anonymity,
Melville ended in a pauper's death.

For thirty years, his masterpiece
lay in the shallows on a few library shelves
until the great American scholar
Carl Van Doren discovered his genius
and brought it to the shore of fame
where it will swim forever.

When I get to Heaven,
I want to be the first to tell Melville
of his glory unless his best friend
Hawthorne beats me to it.

WENDELL BERRY SAID

In his poem, *How To Be A Poet,*
Wendell Berry tells me to sit down and be quiet.
Let my mind breathe.
He lists everything I might bring—
affection, inspiration, patience,
growing older—and says we should doubt
any reader who likes our work.

Write without air-conditioning.
Communicate slowly—there are only
sacred places, nothing unsacred,
but some desecrated places.

I found it on a poetry site I read daily.
Am I the only one who read this Berry poem?
Perhaps if I were sick, I would have missed it.
Perhaps no one else in the world read it.

How many of the eight billion people on Earth
read his intriguing poem today about how to wave
a magic wand and bring verse out of your head
or dross as the day may be?

I will consider his words as I write
a poem today or tomorrow
strutting and fretting my hour upon the page
that perhaps no one will ever read
or a few outside my family

or some retired guy whiling
the time he has left,
honoring what was penned
so long ago.

MEETING FYODOR IN HEAVEN

Though named the laureate only of my street,
I intend to converse with many artists—
a never finished bucket list,
an unending dance card.
Whom would you visit first?

Dostoyevsky, my choice.
I know I'd wait in long lines
unless appointments allowed.

Fyodor and I, so much
in common—except talent.
Like that tortured, inspired writer,
I always seek to discover
if there is divine justice in the universes,
drink my fill of spirits,
mesmerized to perdition
for letting table games
gamble life away,
though I love blackjack,
more than his roulette.

Wayward poet, heretic!
Do I mean to contend that scalawag
would be ceremoniously ushered
through the pearly gates by Peter?
Yes, Fyodor did create
the faithful Alyosha,

decry the moral paucity of Ivan,
the hedonism of Dimitri.

Am I perfect? Be fair even though
it is not our decision at all.
Twain said humans can't judge
a frog-jumping match.

LUBRICATING HISTORY

Liquid coursed through
mountain arteries for centuries,
lubricated the bones
of dinosaurs—Bronto-Quaker,
Saura—Sinclair, Tyrannna—Penz.

Foul, sickening to drink,
could kill you, awful smell.
What use?

Lube for wheels, catapults,
all things squeaking,
once competing with whales.

In recent history,
rapacious use, propelled us
to huge advancements
in rich countries,
petro-chemical empires.

Humans acted human,
greased the skids of history.

We privileged, oil beneficiaries—
friends world-wide, grand vacations,
money to earn as fast as we burn.

Poor Earth: No one asked you
whether to use the ooze.

Drill on, drill deep,
lubricate history to our perdition.

The wheels on the bus
go round and round,
jets zoom, boats motor,
tanks roll, cars speed,
fast enough to crash.

NINETEEN FORTY-FIVE

Tribute to Charles Simic

When my Father left for war,
Mother gave me a wooden Tommy-Gun.
WW II crashed to a close.
Skeletal bodies liberated at Auschwitz.
Hoop Jr. won the Derby.

I leaped behind chairs, killed the enemy,
hoped to bring my Father home.
Audie Murphy awarded the Medal of Honor.
McArthur returned to the Philippines.
Liz stole hearts in National Velvet.

The radio our shrine,
bending our ears in hope.
Hitler married Eva,
suicide for a honeymoon.
VE Day.

My younger brother was born,
almost died in the hospital.
The US seized Iwo Jima.
Army captured college football.
Folic acid discovered in leafy greens.

News of my Dad coming home.
Dancing in the streets.
Steinbeck, Cannery Row,

Wright, Black Boy.
Lucky Strike Hit Parade.

Enola Gay and Boxcar drop the A-bombs.
VJ ends that theater.
Dad returns, kisses Mom a lot.
The Tommy-Gun left on a shelf.
Grand Rapids, first fluoridated water.

Dad and I glued to the radio.
Tigers whip Cubs in World Series,
creates celebration in 2016.
B-52 crashes into Empire State Bldg.,
forecasts 911.

We move into the middle-class,
a washing machine and Oldsmobile.
Wars continue.
I am 79 today.

DECISION

Oh, the heroic pilgrims!,
who chose the Mayflower
when the Speedwell floundered,
off to a new world despite the danger.

Half the saints died that first winter,
but no one chose to return to England.
Instead they set shod feet on Plymouth,
believed God stormed them North,
believed God bequeathed the new land,
to have dominion over and flourish.

But other humans tilled the land,
hunted the pristine forests,
fished the teeming waters.

Given a choice to cooperate in peace,
our ancestors chose
the railroads over the buffalo,
the natives getting in the way.

Sent passenger cars to the herds,
shooting helpless creatures
from open windows,
leaving bodies to rot,
using nothing of value
as the natives preserved all.

Rail-crossed the nation.

Now we dignify our first people
by damning racist mascots,
keep natives the poorest among us.

Our cars cross those tracks—
dirt and iron—
on the way to prosperity.

FRANCE SCOTT KEY REFLECTS ON HIS STAR-SPANGLED BANNER

A Tribute to Colin Kaepernick

Oh, say I can see by the dawn's early light
that our nation won freedom at twilight's last gleaming.
That we declared ourselves the land of the free
despite the millions of slaves we owned.

Oh, say I can see as I stand so proudly,
a brave captive on this British deck
and watch the enemy bomb our fort and flag,
relentlessly pound our freedom into the ground.
I don't notice the slaves that are swimming
desperately towards the British vessels,
don't yet know that a thousand slaves
helped the Redcoats sack our Capitol,
hoping to escape from their American slavers
to the unknown shores of Canada,
believing that Northern freezing clime
will better suit them than our care
for *the hirelings and slaves* we believe
satisfied with our Heaven-rescued land
than any place that has a king.

Oh, say I can see the ignorance
of these people released from African tyranny,
as I opined, "a distinct and inferior race of people,
people who cannot take care of themselves "

if freed and are destined for ruin,
thus kindly I would send them back to Africa.

Oh, say, I see why I chose to lawyer
with my friend Chief Justice Roger Taney to forge
the Dred Scott decision because these ex-slaves
could not take care of themselves.

Oh, say I could not see the Civil War coming,
when my brave Southern states fought
to still enslave these threats to our privilege,
to oppress even after we lost the War,
destroy Reconstruction, fly Jim Crow,
idolize the Klan and keep waving
our Confederate flags right through
Civil Rights and killing King,
as the Party of Lincoln continues
to wave the flag and undermine every effort
to allow these centuries old, oppressed people
the freedom and dignity my anthem celebrated.

KEEP AMERICA GREAT FOREVER.

Colin took a knee.
Millions protest now.

SIGH-N

An older woman now
remembers
Jerome
"Hubba" (because you were)
Norcross
Special Forces Vietnam;
the children
we never had,
the Christmases,
vacations, petty spats;
what you might have become
But didn't….
I think I am glad they mounted
the green memorial sign
noting your sacrifice.
Reminds me to talk to you
every day when I drive to work.

CABARET REVISITED

On the TV news, I watch the faces
of people wearing red hats.
When their hero appears,
they stand at the bar,
raise their beer glasses
in praise. The bartender shrugs,
carefully tops the foam.

The scene reminds me
of the iconic movie *Cabaret,*
when American brat Liza Minelli
charmed the audience,
Joel Grey mastered his *Liebshen*
and mocked the Jewish gorilla.

Nazis terrorized Jews,
killed Frau Landauer's pet dog,
left the bloody corpse,
rang the doorbell,
ran away like
a crude Halloween trick.

As Count Maximilian hustled
Sally in the beer garden, a blond,
blue-eyed Hitler youth rose up,
sang a chilling patriotic song.
O, Fatherland, Fatherland inspired
broken, poor and angry
Germans to stand, join

the rousing tune,
plant their hopes firmly
like a flag for *der Fuhrer.*

The Nazis viciously beat voters
at polls, their uniformed soldiers appear
in eerily greater numbers
filling the final bar scene.

Today, our own frustrated
rise to salute a different tyrant,
recover their pride,
hoping, once again,
to be saved.

O, FATHERLAND, FATHERLAND
MAKE AMERICA GREAT AGAIN!

THE MUSEUM OF HUMAN MISTAKES

I see so many in power
allow the gun murders
to continue unabated, who lie,
argue it is just metallic hearts
not the forged metal of weapons
that cause the Noah's Ark of tears
to flood the world and change nothing.

If these cruel humans
were dragged before crowds,
who can't dance with their children,
heal what can never be healed,
not ever by thoughts and prayers,
repair what cannot be restored,
the genocide of family memories,
the terror of children who lie
in bed thinking they might be next,

I would be cheering,
celebrating the demise
of those who would not listen,
would not change, glorying in a future
where their guns did not exist,
guns into plowshares or, more modern,
melted into computers to learn
by the children still left, guns exhibited
in The Museum Of Human Mistakes.

IF NOTHING IS DONE

Can a human be a drop in the bucket of history,
a tiny ping in a vast cistern, but jump in anyway?

In WW II, Witold Pileki, officer
in the Polish Underground,
hounded his commanders to allow
him to join Polish Jews sent to Auschwitz,
suspected something dreadful in that camp,
left his wife and two small children.

Arm-inked #4859, he discovered the atrocities.
For three years, smuggled reports
in dirty laundry to the outside,
every basket a chance for capture.
He knew what the prison guards did to spies.

His reports: gas chambers, ovens
to the Polish Underground.
Sent those atrocities to Americans and British.
No one believed.
No one would do such things!

We have a history of things done,
not a history of things not done.
How many would have been saved
if someone had listened?

Waited, arranged escapes for prisoners,
but nothing done. Frustrated,

faked typhus and escaped himself.
Spied against Russia till the Reds killed him.

We call so many heroes—tycoons, doctors,
baseball players, astronauts.
Is Witold still a hero
if nothing is done?

OLD TRICKS

In our apartment building,
when I was a child,
old Mrs. Greta Shultz horrified me.
We lived by an airport,
every whining sound of jets
sent that creaky lady
scuttling under the kitchen table,
duck and cover every time,
air sucked in, moans—
for her an American *Luftwaffe,*
Slaughterhouse Dresden memories—
her mind recoiling
at the screaming sounds
from her younger girl day/nightmares.
Despite heart-felt pleas,
Greta was safe under the table.

After years of marriage,
we rescued a dog.
She had been caged
for months in cold wire.
We gave her our warm and safe home.
But when my wife ever went out,
Butter would mewl by the door,
shiver and shake
till the door opened,
de-plane on my wife's lap.
No coaxing mattered.

You can't unlearn old tricks.

DEATH SPEAKS TO YOU

Sorry to intrude into your young world.
You may ignore me.
I am not sure why I am telling you this,
but Death does begin to speak to you
at a certain age,
probably different for everyone.
I am near 80, she, he, it—
Death has no personna
except what we invent—
mine a scythe wielding crone
with a hideous grin—
just starts to remind,
whispers in my ear
not all the time,
just at a dark corner,
at a crosswalk,
at the top of the stairs,
any time of day or night
in dreams, daymares,
before the morning pills,
before I snap on
the electric blanket.

Death says
a bone pain here,
an ache there,
what you did,
what you didn't do,
a slight fever,

a newspaper article,
FaceBook stab,
TV bray,
a small limp,
a sudden fall,
whispers, whispers,
perhaps nags.
I suspect Death
will not stop
or go away
until we do.

HUMAN BITES

A mosquito is born, a human is born.
Both destined to die.
The mosquito does not know this.
Mosquitoes will never think on it,
no concept of prevention.
The insect will just do its blood thing and die.
That is the difference between the two.

The human seldom thinks of death.
Eventually, the human accepts reality.
When he does, he doesn't want to die.
He is against dying but realizes
it's a futile thought, a deceptive myth,
numbs himself with myriad palliatives—
an apothecary shelf of addictions.

Why do humans, who know they will die,
devise so many ways to kill each other?
The mosquito might give you a better answer.

A SUBTLE TRIBULATION

If you have pored over Revelation,
nothing subtle there.
Destruction on every level,
unprecedented pain and suffering.
The one world government begats
the great world war begats
inflation and famine begats
a mighty earthquake, hide under rocks
begats a third of trees and grass burn up
begats blood rains down begats
a mountain of sulphur falls in the sea
begats the Star Wormwood,
bitters the sea
begats a diminished sun, moon, stars,
brings ever darkness begats
scorpions and locusts cause men
to plead for death begats
the Vial Judgments,
as God destroys all human systems,
ends Babylon in agony.

Maybe instead of a cataclysm,
a spectacular, big bang disaster,
the Tribulation is now,
happening before my very eyes,
day by night?

Daily I see the cracks,
shootings, bombings,

violence everywhere,
environmental fires,
collapsing ice bergs,
nuclear warheads bristling,
pandemics raging against the bit,
refugees aswarm
as nation wars against nation
kings more insane,
the rich so far above
the unseen poor,
a mist at the foot
of their mountain strongholds.

For myself, a privileged one,
a first world denizen,
so much good still:
An unruffled life:
Family vacations,
celebrate birthdays,
root for my teams,
my wife plants her garden,
new marriages, new babies.
I get up in the morning,
brush my teeth,
sleep tired.
So much good.

I go though my daily life,
not knowing what to do,
cluck my tongue more and more
as the news accosts me,
like a Marathon runner
daily falling exhausted at my feet,

as he reports event after event.
Toffler warned us—
media unleashed would
overwhelm us,
an impending sense of doom,
a feeling the other shoe
of the world will drop.

The evil increases.
I can feel it
as the Tribulation
drips, drips,
a rivulet, a stream,
a river, an ocean,
tsunami without end,
man clawing at himself
in abject fear,
clutching at what
will not hold still.

CUP RUNNETH OVER

In ancient Israel
the holy men
collected tears
in a special cup,
every time they laughed,
mostly when they cried.

As life struck their hearts
and the tears flowed,
they would catch them
in their holy cup
until it runneth over
and in those hard times
with some merriment
the cup runneth over
so that the blessings from God
were not why they said:
My cup runneth over
but because
they had human hearts full
of sorrow and compassion
and sometimes great joy,
an offering,
blessings for who they were
and not for what they expected
and only some,
hopefully very few,
had neither a cup
nor many blessings.
Amen.

BILLY THE KID IN HEAVEN

"The Kid is here,"
said Peter to Paul:
"A poor boy, never had a chance.
His life—chance.
Don't you remember ours, Paul?
Your road to Damascus.
Me, the cock crowing, three times."

Catherine, his mother,
moved to Wichita, hell town.
Raised Henry, battled TB,
died in New Mexico.
Her scalawag husband
fled to New Mexico
for gold and gamble.

Alone, Henry, fifteen,
stole butter to sell for food.
The Sherriff let him go.
Clothes to cover himself
from a Chinese laundry.
Landlady sent him to jail.
Escaped, one of many.

Couldn't find a job,
fell into crime, rustling.
Pat Garrett arrested Billy,
escaped again.
Garrett chased him down,
shot him in the back.

People said—*fine looking a young man*
you ever met, winning smile,
good dancer, ladies' man.

"Yes, he qualifies," said Peter.
"He had a hard life.
I'll be proud to know him.
Paul, put him in the line
with the forgiven
who never had a chance."

THE UN-CHOSEN

The Chosen people
un-chosen for one night.
Huddled in the dark
no fire
listened for wings
any rustle
prayed for lamb's blood
to protect them
from the Angel of Death.

Did they hear the wails
clutch their first born
in the middle of the night?

The Chosen people
un-chosen one time,
blessed.

THEOLOGY

You say there is no Heaven.
Fly with me now
across the world
to a breast
in one country,
as long as the people
are starving,
it does not matter where.
A desiccated breast.
Sere.
Clinging, an infant,
boy or girl?
Doesn't matter.
Sucking scarce milk from a drying teat,
soon to die,
like its siblings,
like its mother.
Doesn't matter.
You say there is no Heaven.
You say there is no justice.
The universe just happened,
by accident,
just appeared,
exploding into beautiful, us.

Outcomes just came out.

Okay.
Fly back with me,

back to our country,
to a crib in the suburbs.
See my niece,
dressed in pink,
a silver spoon in her mouth.
She will live to a ripe old age,
have a beau,
have a baby,
maybe more for the nanny.
Boys or girls,
doesn't matter.
A plump, full breast
or Silk milk.
You say:
Too bad, too bad!
It's just too bad.
That's just the way
the cookie crumbles in the milk.
I don't think about the future, Heaven.
Doesn't matter.
I can't think about those other babies.

Hand me a fresh diaper.
Hurry, I have to go,
meeting my hubby at the restaurant.
Hurry.

WHEN THE FIRST LEAF FELL

When there were first trees,
we know they leafed,
still leaf and leave.

When that first leaf fell,
a universal sigh rose,
an Earth-shattering groan;
trees threw their branches up in horror.

Despite its beautiful colors,
green face painted with orange and brown
when the first leaf twisted and wafted down,
did the trees feel what was coming,
know the cycle of seasons began,
death trailing birth forever?

The first leaves fell
and Autumn appeared
after the Fall.

SPIKE OF LIGHT

He woke up in the dark and knew.
He already knew but now New
touched His face, moved His head
slightly to the left, opened His eyes,
a crack of dawn, a tiny crack of dawn
spiked from the tomb door soon
footsteps and He knew his own
would walk eternally with the others.

FISHING

On the way, we took a wrong turn.
We will catch and clean certain fish instead of others.

NOBODY DIED

Whenever the shit hits the fan
you crash the car,
our TV and washing machine go kaput the same week,
our daughter gets fired
our grandsons move to Montana.

How long do you have to hear our woes?

We often say to each other,
as a way to staunch the angst:
"Nobody died. Nobody died."

That causes us to stop our complaining,
look at each other,
realize the worst tragedies did not happen to us.
As our minds comb through the tangled hair of others' lives.
Indeed, some bodies did die.

We have friends who lost children,
the ultimate God Forbid—three genetic cancers and a drug overdose.
Did you ever look into the eyes of a mother who lost her eldest daughter?

We are aware of the world, the terrible storms across the globe
Biblical earthquakes and famines, birth pang beginnings, the moon turns to blood

the predictable suicide bombings, escalating mass shootings,
unfathomable beheadings

the incessant wars nagging at our peace everyday
wars and rumors of wars, nation against nation

the widening poverty the rich glee in

the local teen selling popcorn at the football concession stand
paid with a stray bullet

media responsibly bringing the bad news
as if it were some perpetual Marathon runner
falling exhausted before our brains every day.

Oh, the world is too much with us, late and soon, getting and spending, we lay waste our powers: Little we see in Nature that is ours,
Wordsworth lamented.

We don't say any of this.
We always end
with that litany of solace,
"Nobody died,"
which is true for us,
FOR NOW.

DESPITE:
OF HANSEL AND GRETEL'S WITCH

A bone bent rag pile
before the Pearly Gates
waits for the Saint
to pass judgment,
broods on forgiveness.

One says she knows not what she did,
but she did build the candy house
—lemon cookie walls, chocolate windows,
red and green Christmas candy roof, apple pie porch—
like a predator on a playground,
peeps out for any sign
of fattling children.

Her natural witch clairvoyance
knew they were coming,
Hansel's bread crumb scheme,
snatched away by the birds
as she would tempt them
then slam the purple candy door
and pop him in her cage.

Smart children, honed
by the step-mothers's wiles,
Gretel devises
the twig finger
to out-trick the tricker.

Day by day, the crone's eyes
see wood instead of flesh,
impossible to wait
for succulence,
orders Gretel:
Light the oven,
carrots and gravy,
bake the boy.
Stupidly bends over
to test the heat,
whoosh the witch
into the fire.

The children flee home,
find their kind woodcutter father.
Bring baskets of goodies,
celebrate love and family.

The stepmother banished,
the children see her once more—
buy her bread and soup—
despite.

I'M SORRY

We say to the animate world.
We have inflicted so much hurt
on other humans—even the ones we most love.
We neglect a dog, a cat, a horse,
leave a bird cage ajar, stomp bugs.
We have not been St. Francis.
Sorry, a healing balm.

But what of the inanimate world?
Some say plants feel pain
when we yank them from the ground,
routinely murder the lawn.
We can kneel down
in our own garden
or by our mower and say it.
And, lumberjack—apologize to that tree
you just axed.

What about convenience items?
When they break, we bitch
even when we break them.
Like it was their fault.
Hey, if you buy 47 things
with moving parts, the law of averages
says at least two a week will break.
When you cuss out your furnace
or TV—humble yourself.

Do you stomp the floor
when you stub your toe?
Do you kick a chair
when you bang into it?
You put it there.
Or the table you bump,
the sidewalk that scrapes your knee.
Teach your children early on,
extend the chain of life to the lifeless.

Could be life changing,
apologizing not just to the living,
breathing world,
but to every
thing.

Like to your bed for not making it every day,
letting her live a rumpled life.
Like your toilet some still call a commode.
Sorry for all the shit you have to put up with.

Mea Culpa—to all the rocks I threw.

MODERN DAY GLADIATORS: A MODEST PROPOSAL

Hey fans, I'm sick of these barnburners.
heart-attack endings, last shot nightmares,
even if your team wins, blood pressure rises,
hearts palpitate, way too much stress.
All you have to look forward to is the next game.
Two hours of agony till the last second shot.
Enough.

Let's do it like the gladiators of old,
mano a mano, David and Goliath,
some whole wars decided that way.
Each selected the best warriors.
The winners vanquished the others' army.
Everyone went home to his family
after one side buried their dead guy.
The fight didn't take that long, maybe a whole day,
even into the night, or the speed
it takes for a stone to hit a forehead.

We could do that in basketball,
maybe other sports too.
Line up the teams, each gets the ball to score
until one does and one doesn't.

Then many more games, short stress,
the whole tourney in a few days.
Go get a beer with your buddies
and cry or cheer till the next short joust.

BIRDSONG

I woke up this morning
when the birds sang.
The tweet and the trill,
the peep peep, the usual chirps.
God's alarm clock.

But this one morning,
grating songs,
raucous sounds,
needling sharp notes,
obnoxious squacks
like never before.

Ran to the window,
squinted down the sun,
alert for the danger,
the disturbance
that would turn melody
into ear-covering noise,
an atonal avian symphony.

But there was no danger.
The birds had abandoned
their sweet songs—
annoying, threatening, cacophonous—
Keats' nightmare, not nightingale.
The noise would have driven
the couple stark out of Eden.

The wren's warble, a red-breasted song.
A caw is melodious,
even the bluejay's screech
can be beautiful.

Oh, never take for granted
delightful bird song.

WHAT DOES WATER HEAR?

Falls in sprinkles or violent storms,
runs in rivulets, streams, settles in ponds—
live or stagnant—rivers, seas, oceans—
does water listen?

What does it hear?
Parched cry of the ground.
Oasis prayer.
Rocks beg for smooth
erosion to eternity.
Human plea for quench.
Animals gulp, slurp.
Children splash in hose fun.
Smack of children's water balloons.
Drip drip of the waiting faucet.
Flush we want and don't want to hear.
Sound of waves on the shore's lap,
breaks fiercely on the rocks.
Roar of falls, white water.
Whoosh of a whale's spout.
Gentle showers on the evening garden.
Water exclaims into wine.
Sipping a cup of cold water saves a soul.

Water, water everywhere,
less and less to drink.

Listen to the water.

REFLECTION ON DOTS

Whenever I see we are
one
of millions of galaxies,
I feel like a dot of a dot of a dot.

No feelings or memories in galaxies.

No galaxy married the most beautiful other dot in the world,
birthed three other dots with that dot,
stood looking out at its own raging, blue ocean,
sad that one dot spoke terrible things about another dot,
voted for one dot over another,
wondered why one dot only ate vegetables, another meat.

Or was horrified when a dot crashed his car into another dot,
gazed at the big white dots in the black sky,
amazed as dots created music, paintings,
poems, novels, sculptures,
scorned a dot of a different color,
warmed to a dot rescuing a dog,
felt the distant dot of a red, pulsing sun.

Or marveled as a dot explored an unknown sunset-soaked vista,
spied one dot stealing from another,
shot a basketball through a dot on a pole,
cheered when a dot carried a picket sign,
exclaimed when a dot danced with lotto winnings from dots on a
ticket,
cried as one dot adulterized a dot's dot.

Or scaled the dot of a mountain,
lauded a dot for the sonnet she wrote,
screamed as a drunken dot jumped off a bridge,
contemplated dots supplicating, genuflecting, meditating,
surveyed a placid, green lake with an egret dot,
loved a dot petting a swan, another petting a bull.

Or dropped bombs on other dots.

Or looked up, realized
had one of those dots
left her other dots far too early
we would look up at those other galaxies
and know that dot
was somewhere out there.

Acknowledgements

Grateful acknowledgement is made to the editors of the following journals in which many of these poems first appeared.

—WORDS AND WHISPERS
—UPPAGUS
—THE LITERARY YARD, TERROR HOUSE MAGAZINE, THE DAILY DRUNK HUMOR MAGAZINE, THE BEZINE, TRASH TO TREASURES
—SPANK THE CARP, SILENT SPARK, STICK FIGURE MAGAZINE, SANCTUARY MAGAZINE, SPINDRIFT, SOFT CARTEL
—RAT'S ASS REVIEW
—PAPER CROW, POESIS MAGAZINE, POETICA REVIEW, POETRY AND COVID
—ODD BALL MAGAZINE
—MONTEREY POETRY REVIEW
—LOTHLORIEN JOURNAL
—IBIS HEAD REVIEW
—HEART OF FLESH
—GREY SPARROW JOURNAL, GREEN SILK JOURNAL, GOLD DUST MAGAZINE
—FLEAS ON THE DOG
—EUPHEMISM MAGAZINE
—DOWN IN THE DIRT MAGAZINE
—CORVUS REVIEW, COMMUNICATOR'S LEAGUE, COURTSHIP OF WINDS
—BINDWEED MAGAZINE, BOMBFIRE MAGAZINE, BLUE PEPPER MAGAZINE. BROADKILL REVIEW, BEYOND THESE SHORES
—AGAPE REVIEW

www.ingramcontent.com/pod-product-compliance
Lightning Source LLC
Chambersburg PA
CBHW050019170726
48282CB00025B/461
* 9 7 8 8 1 1 9 2 2 8 0 7 2 *